Social Stories for Kids with PDA Autism

Gentle Tales that Ease Anxiety, From
Overwhelm to Understanding

Rowan Arlen G.

Dedication

For the brave ones whose "no" is not defiance, whose silence is not emptiness, and whose difference is their greatest strength.

Table of Content

4

Introduction

To the Parent, Caregiver, or Teacher Holding This Book

It started with a shoe.

One morning, the shoe just would not go on. Not the left one, not the right. The laces were "too stringy." The socks felt "too spiky." The hallway light was "too bright." Breakfast had the "wrong smell." And school? School felt like a monster waiting outside the front door.

The child—beautiful, bright, and brilliant—curled up on the floor, unable to move. The adult—exhausted, confused, loving, trying—sat beside them, unsure of what to say next. Not angry. Not helpless. Just… lost in the storm.

If you have ever lived this moment—something small becoming impossibly big—you are in the right place.

This book was made for you. And more importantly, for your child.

What This Book Is

This is not just a book of stories.

This is a collection of gentle moments. Real-life challenges—like change, demand, anxiety, sound, transitions—told through the eyes of one child who, like many with PDA autism, sees the world a little differently.

You will meet Riley—not a boy, not a girl, just a child—who sometimes struggles with things that others might find easy. Riley teaches us that it is okay to say no, it is okay to feel big things, and it is possible to find calm, even when the world feels like too much.

Why Social Stories?

Children with Pathological Demand Avoidance (PDA) often experience the world in intense, unpredictable ways.

Demands—even gentle ones—can trigger deep anxiety. Routines offer safety. Sudden changes, emotional expectations, or unclear social rules can lead to overwhelm.

Social stories help by gently introducing these situations, giving children a safe script to follow, and showing them that they are not wrong, just wired differently. They also give adults a way to talk about these tough moments without blame, fear, or force.

How to Use This Book

- Read each story slowly, at your child's pace.

- Use the same tone each time—it helps build trust.

- If a story feels too much, pause. Try again later.

- Talk about Riley like a friend: "What do you think Riley felt here?"

- Let your child reflect, connect, and grow at their own rhythm.

This is not a quick fix. It is a soft journey.

One where overwhelm slowly gives way to understanding.

One story at a time.

A Final Word

You are not alone.

Your child is not broken.

And this journey—while not easy—is full of beauty, bravery, and breakthroughs.

So take a deep breath.

Hold this book with kindness.

And let the stories begin.

Story 1: Riley and the Big Morning Storm

Anxiety, Morning Routine Disruption, Sensory Overload

Riley liked mornings to go the same way every day.

Wake up. Blue socks. Cereal with exactly three strawberries. Then the green jacket, not the red one. And finally, sit by the window until the school bus honked exactly two times.

That was Riley's morning. Safe. Predictable. Calm.

But today, something was different.

The blue socks were missing.

"Where are they?" Riley asked, voice starting to rise.

"We'll find them later. Just wear the red ones today," said the grown-up, calmly.

Red ones? RED? Riley's stomach started flipping. The red socks felt too tight. Too itchy. Too wrong.

"No," Riley said, louder now. "I can't wear those."

The grown-up knelt down, soft voice ready. "What if we try to breathe first?"

But Riley was already feeling it—the storm inside. A big, loud, twisty feeling climbing up and up and up.

Then the cereal was wrong too.

Only two strawberries. And one of them had a soft spot.

"No. No. No!" Riley cried, pushing the bowl away. The table shook.

"Riley," the grown-up said gently, "this morning is feeling hard, isn't it?"

Riley could not speak. Could not even look up.

Everything felt wrong. Everything felt huge. The socks. The strawberries. The sun shining through the window. Even the noise of the bus outside felt like thunder.

The grown-up sat beside Riley and didn't say anything for a while.

Just stayed there. Breathing slowly.

Then they said, "Would you like your calm corner?"

Riley gave a small nod.

In the corner of Riley's room was a soft blanket, a squishy ball, and a picture of clouds. That was Riley's calm space.

Riley sat down, hugging the squishy ball tight. Breathing in. Breathing out.

Riley finds their calm space — quiet, soft, and safe.

The storm inside started to slow down.

"Today was not how you expected," said the grown-up later. "That can be really hard."

Riley nodded, slowly.

"But guess what?" the grown-up continued. "You found your calm. You rode the storm. And you're still here."

Riley smiled. Just a little.

Story 2: The Day Riley Did Not Want to Get Dressed

Sensory Overload, Autonomy, and Saying No Safely

Riley woke up feeling a little tight inside.

Not tight like a squeeze, but tight like a balloon stretched too full — like one more thing might make everything pop.

Today was a school day. Riley usually liked school. But not always the getting-ready part.

"Time to get dressed," the grown-up called from the hallway.

Riley stared at the shirt on the bed. It was soft. It was clean. It was blue — Riley's favorite color.

But it still felt... wrong.

Riley touched the sleeve. Too crinkly.

Riley touched the collar. Too scratchy.

"I don't want to wear this," Riley whispered.

The grown-up peeked in. "What's up, Riley?"

Riley shook their head. The tight feeling was getting tighter.

The grown-up walked over, picked up the shirt, and said gently, "Okay. Let's think together. What part doesn't feel right?"

Riley pressed their fingers to their temples. "It feels like… it's fighting me."

The grown-up smiled softly. "Then it's not the one for today. Want to look through your comfort drawer?"

Riley nodded. The comfort drawer had clothes that never argued — soft shirts, loose pants, tag-free socks. Clothes that felt like a hug.

Riley chose a big grey hoodie and soft shorts. They looked a little funny together, but Riley's body didn't care. The storm began to settle.

While Riley got dressed, the grown-up said something quietly:

"You are allowed to say no to things that do not feel right to your body."

Riley turned slowly. "Really?"

"Really," the grown-up said. "It's your body. It should feel safe in what it wears."

Later that morning, Riley zipped up their hoodie and smiled.

They were dressed.

They were comfortable.

They were ready in their own way.

And that was more than enough.

Story 3: Riley's Bubble of Calm

Emotional Regulation and Creating a Safe Space

Some days, Riley could feel the day before it even started.

It would be one of those days — the kind where the world felt too loud, too fast, and too full.

The air felt heavy. The sounds seemed sharper. Even breakfast had too many smells.

Riley did not know why it happened. It just did.

The grown-up noticed.

They always noticed.

"Want to talk?" they asked softly.

Riley shook their head. Talking felt like too many words.

The grown-up nodded. "Okay. Want your calm bubble instead?"

That got a little nod.

The calm bubble was not a real bubble. Not like soap bubbles.

It was something Riley imagined.

It started at their feet — a soft circle of safety growing around them. It moved slowly, gently, like warm light wrapping Riley in quiet.

Inside their invisible bubble, Riley could breathe and think — a quiet place they built all by themselves.

Inside the bubble, everything slowed down.

The sounds outside became softer.

The lights stopped buzzing.

The pressure in Riley's chest eased.

The grown-up helped sometimes.

They would whisper:

"Breathe in, Riley... one, two, three."

"Breathe out... slow like clouds."

Then they would sit close, but not too close. No talking. Just being there.

Riley closed their eyes. Inside the bubble, Riley could think.

They thought about clouds. About wind. About trees that swayed but did not fall.

And in that moment, the world was still too much—but Riley was okay inside the bubble.

Later that day, when things got loud again, Riley whispered something:

"I'm going back to my bubble."

The grown-up smiled. "That's your superpower."

And it was.

Because Riley had something special—not everyone could build a calm place inside themselves.

But Riley could.

And that meant Riley could always find peace again.

Even when the world felt too big.

Story 4: Riley and the Lunchbox Mix-Up

Handling Surprises, Change, and Regaining Control

Lunchtime was Riley's favorite part of the school day.

Not because of the food, really —
though the triangle-cut sandwiches
were always nice — but because lunch
meant predictability. Riley always knew
what would be in the box: crackers,
cheese, sliced apples, and one chewy
chocolate chip cookie.

It was packed just right, smelled just
right, and tasted exactly the way Riley
needed it to.

But today, something was wrong.

When Riley opened the lunchbox, they froze.

The sandwich wasn't triangle-cut — it was whole.

There were no crackers. No apple slices.

And worst of all… no cookie.

Just carrots. A squished banana. And a sandwich with mustard — mustard!

Riley's eyes widened. Their throat tightened. It felt like the room had suddenly tilted sideways.

"I think this isn't mine," Riley said, voice trembling.

Their friend, Theo, looked over. "You sure?"

Riley nodded. Their hands were starting to sweat. The world was starting to blur.

The smell of mustard felt like it was crawling up their nose.

"I can't eat this," Riley whispered.

The grown-up on duty noticed Riley's shoulders scrunching up.

They knelt beside Riley, speaking slowly.

"Hey, I see this is different today. Looks like someone's lunches got switched."

Riley could not answer.

The world inside their body was spinning. The air felt thick. The quiet hum of the cafeteria turned into roaring noise.

"It's okay if this feels hard," the grown-up said. "Would you like to step outside for a minute?"

Riley gave a small, fast nod. They clutched their lunchbox like it might fall apart and followed the grown-up into the hallway

When the world felt upside down, Riley found comfort in a quiet hallway — and someone who truly listened.

Once they sat on the bench, the grown-up took a deep breath and waited. No questions. No pressure. Just quiet.

After a moment, they said, "I think your lunch got switched with Jamie's. Yours is still in the fridge. Want me to go grab it?"

Riley didn't answer right away.

Instead, they stared at the wall, trying to slow the waves inside their body.

They wanted to scream. They wanted to cry.

But most of all, they wanted the world to make sense again.

"Can I still eat outside?" Riley asked softly.

The grown-up smiled. "Of course."

A few minutes later, Riley sat in the sunshine with the right lunchbox in their lap.

Triangle sandwich. Crackers. Apple slices. And that chewy cookie.

The storm had passed — not because nothing went wrong, but because Riley had been given time, space, and choice.

Later that evening, Riley told the grown-up at home, "It wasn't a good day… but it wasn't a bad one either."

And for Riley, that meant the day had been a win.

Because even when the plan falls apart, safety can still be found.

Sometimes all it takes is someone who listens… and a triangle sandwich to bring the world back into balance.

Story 5: When Riley Wanted to Stay at the Park Forever

Transitioning from Enjoyed Activities and Respecting Emotional Limits

The swing moved back and forth, back and forth, like waves on a quiet beach.

Riley's eyes were half-closed, face turned to the wind, arms stretched wide like a bird gliding through the sky.

The park was Riley's favorite place — especially the swing.

It was just right.

Not loud. Not crowded.

The sky was blue, the breeze was soft, and the swing never asked anything of Riley.

The grown-up sat on a bench nearby, smiling.

It had been a good day — no shoes-too-tight moments, no surprise smells, no unexpected demands. Just peace. Just the swing.

Until the grown-up stood up and called out, "Five more minutes, Riley!"

And just like that, something inside Riley snapped.

Riley's legs stopped moving. The swing slowed. The wind felt colder now.

"Five minutes?" Riley said, panicked. "Why? I don't want to leave!"

The grown-up walked over. "We talked about going to Grandma's house after the park, remember?"

"I don't care!" Riley shouted. "I want to stay here! I need to stay here!"

Sometimes leaving something good is the hardest part — but Riley was learning how to say goodbye in their own way.

Their voice cracked like a lightning bolt through the air.

The grown-up stayed calm, crouching beside the swing.

"I know this is your favorite place. And I know it's hard to stop doing something when it feels this good."

Riley's fists clenched. The tears were already gathering in their eyes.

"It's not fair," Riley whispered. "Everything else is hard. This is the only thing that feels right."

The grown-up didn't argue. They nodded slowly.

"Okay," they said. "How about this: we take one more minute to make a goodbye plan. Then we do it together."

Riley blinked. "A goodbye plan?"

"Yes. What's one way you can say goodbye to the swing so your body feels a little better?"

Riley thought for a moment, still shaky. Then they said, "Two big pushes. Then I'll touch the pole. Then I'll say 'See you next time.'"

The grown-up nodded. "That sounds like a perfect plan."

Riley gave two powerful swings.

Touched the pole gently.

Then whispered, "See you next time."

It still felt sad. But it did not feel impossible anymore.

And when Riley walked away, hand in the grown-up's hand, they looked back once and smiled.

Because leaving something good is always hard.

But Riley learned something new that day.

When you get to say goodbye your own way, it makes space for the next good thing to come.

Story 6: Riley's First Dentist Adventure

Fear of the Unknown, Sensory Overload, and Gentle Preparation

Riley had never been to the dentist before.

Not once.

And now, there was an appointment circled in red on the calendar.

Riley stared at it like it was a monster in disguise.

"Why do I have to go?" Riley asked.

The grown-up smiled gently. "To keep your teeth strong. But we can talk about it first."

Riley frowned. "I don't like places I don't know."

The grown-up had a plan.

They showed Riley a picture of the dentist's office. Not real people — just a drawing with soft colors.

"There's a big chair that leans back," the grown-up said. "It feels like flying."

"Do they poke you?" Riley asked.

"They look at your teeth with a tiny mirror," said the grown-up. "And they wear gloves. You can even bring something that makes you feel safe."

Riley thought for a long time. Then packed their "Adventure Kit":

- Noise-canceling headphones

- A soft hoodie with a deep hood

- A small stuffed turtle named Cloudy

- And a card with calming words: You are safe. You are brave. You can stop and ask for space.

The day came. Riley's stomach felt like jelly.

The waiting room had a funny smell — kind of like soap and mint and something else. Riley squeezed Cloudy tight.

When the hygienist called their name, Riley's legs felt like stone.

But the grown-up placed a hand on Riley's shoulder and whispered, "We go slow. You're in charge."

Inside, the dentist smiled and didn't speak too fast. "Hi Riley. We're just going to count your teeth today. No poking. No scary stuff. Sound okay?"

Riley nodded — just once.

The dentist noticed Riley's headphones and gave a thumbs-up. "Those are cool. We'll keep everything quiet for you."

Riley got in the chair, still tense, but curious.

They didn't like the bright light — so the grown-up held up a towel as a shade.

The tools made noises — but the headphones helped.

And when it was done, the dentist said, "Great job. You were the boss the whole time."

Riley smiled a little.

Not because they loved it.

Not because it was easy.

But because they did something brave — on their own terms.

And that day, Riley learned something important:

Scary things do not always stay scary —

especially when people go slow, listen close,

and let you be the boss of your own body.

Story 7: Riley Does Not Want to Say Hello

Social Pressure, Autonomy, and Finding Safe Ways to Connect

Riley liked people — just not all the time.

Sometimes, seeing someone new or familiar was okay.

Other times, even looking at someone's face felt like walking into the sun with no sunglasses.

Today, Riley and the grown-up were walking into a friend's house.

The door opened.

"Hi, Riley!" the friend's mom said brightly.

Riley froze.

Riley's hands went into their hoodie pocket. Their eyes stayed glued to the floor. Their shoulders tightened.

The grown-up leaned down and whispered, "Do you want to wave, nod, or skip it for now?"

Riley didn't move.

"I just want to go inside," Riley whispered.

The grown-up nodded and looked at the friend's mom.

*Riley didn't speak — but their grown-up did,
and that made all the difference.*

"She's not ready to say hello right now,
but she's happy to be here."

The friend's mom smiled and stepped
aside. "No problem at all."

Inside the house, Riley's heart was still thumping.

"Why do people need me to say hi?" they asked softly once they were alone with the grown-up.

The grown-up sat beside them. "Some people like greetings because it feels friendly. But not everyone is ready for that kind of moment."

Riley frowned. "I don't want to be rude. I just… can't always do it."

The grown-up nodded. "That's okay. You don't have to say words to be kind. Your presence is already a hello."

Later that afternoon, Riley was feeling calmer.

They picked up a marker and drew a picture of the house. Then, on the back, they wrote:

Thank you for letting me play today.

And gave it to the friend's mom before they left.

The mom smiled. "This means a lot, Riley."

Riley didn't say anything.

But they gave a tiny wave.

That was enough.

Because kindness comes in many shapes —

and Riley had the right to choose their own way of saying "I'm here, and I care."

Even if it did not come out as a word.

Story 8: Riley and the Loud Birthday Party

Sensory Overload, Emotional Safety, and Self-Advocacy in Social Settings

Riley was invited to Zoe's birthday party.

There were balloons on the invite. Cupcakes. Games. A piñata.

At first, it sounded exciting. Riley liked Zoe. They liked cake. They even liked watching piñatas explode (from a distance).

But the day of the party, Riley's stomach had other plans.

It flopped. It turned. It whispered: What if it's too loud? Too bright? Too many people?

The grown-up noticed.

"You don't have to stay the whole time," they said. "Let's make an exit plan and a quiet signal."

Riley nodded slowly. That helped.

In their backpack, Riley packed essentials:

- Noise-reducing headphones

- A small flashlight in case the lights got weird

- Their hoodie

- A tiny fidget cube

- And a card that said: I need a break. Please do not talk to me right now.

When they got to the party, Riley's eyes blinked fast.

There were bright streamers. Kids shouting. A giant speaker playing music with lots of bass. The piñata swung from a tree, already laughing in rainbow colors.

Zoe ran up. "Riley! Come on! We're about to play a game!"

Riley smiled — sort of. "I'm going to just look for a bit first."

Zoe nodded and ran off. That made Riley feel better.

Inside, Riley found a beanbag in a corner of the porch. The grown-up handed them headphones and whispered, "This can be your base spot. Want me to stay close?"

While the party went on, Riley made their own space — quieter, safer, just right.

Riley nodded.

Later, the games started. The shouting grew louder. The balloon popped — and Riley jumped so high they dropped their fidget cube.

The grown-up caught Riley's eyes and held up their hand, like a question.

Riley held up their card silently.

The grown-up led them gently to the car. "You did great," they said.

"But I did not stay the whole time," Riley muttered.

"You stayed for what your body could handle," the grown-up replied. "That is success."

That evening, Zoe's mom sent a message:

Riley was so thoughtful. Tell them thank you for coming. I loved their quiet wave and their drawing.

Riley read the message twice. Then smiled into their pillow.

Because sometimes, being part of the fun means knowing your limits —

and stepping out before it all becomes too much is not quitting.

It is wisdom.

And Riley had plenty of that.

Story 9: When Riley Does Not Want to Play

Boundaries, Emotional Awareness, and Respecting Autonomy

At school, Riley liked to play — sometimes.

They liked stacking blocks by color. They liked drawing long maps of made-up lands. They liked sitting beside friends quietly, not always talking, just being.

But today, Riley did not want to play.

Not with blocks.

Not with friends.

Not with anyone.

Theo came over with a toy car. "Wanna race?"

Riley shook their head. "Not right now."

"Why not?" Theo asked, frowning. "You always like racing."

"I just don't want to today," Riley whispered.

Some days, Riley needed space — not because they didn't care, but because their body said 'not now.

Theo stared at them. "Are you mad at me?"

"No," Riley said quickly. "I just… my body says no."

Theo didn't get it. "But I brought your favorite car!"

Riley stood up and walked to the corner of the classroom, where the beanbag was.

The teacher noticed.

She came over softly. "Hey Riley, are you okay?"

Riley hugged their knees. "I'm not mad. I just need quiet. But Theo thinks I don't like him."

"Want me to help explain?" the teacher asked.

Riley nodded slowly.

The teacher knelt beside Theo and said, "Riley's having a low-energy day. You know how sometimes your body wants to run, and sometimes it wants to rest? Riley's body is resting right now."

Theo looked confused. "So they don't hate me?"

"Not at all," the teacher smiled. "Riley's just listening to their own needs. That's actually something pretty strong."

Later, Theo sat beside Riley on the beanbag — not too close.

He held out the car.

"You don't have to race. But maybe we can just hold them together."

Riley smiled a little. "That's okay."

So they sat. Quiet. Not racing.

Just two friends holding cars.

And that was more than enough.

Because real friendship does not mean doing everything together.

Sometimes it means understanding someone's quiet "no" —

and sitting beside them anyway.

Story 10: Riley and the Big Change at School

Unexpected Change, Trust, and Emotional Recovery

Riley loved the reading corner at school.

It had a soft green rug, pillows shaped like stars, and shelves lined with books that smelled like paper and magic. Most importantly, it had Mrs. Ada — Riley's teacher, the one with warm hands and a calm voice that never rushed.

But one morning, everything changed.

When Riley walked in, the rug was gone.

The pillows were gone.

And standing in Mrs. Ada's place was someone new — a woman with sharp glasses and too much energy in her smile.

"Good morning!" she said brightly. "I'm Ms. Jenna, your guest teacher for today!"

Riley didn't answer. Their eyes scanned the room.

Where was the rug?

Where was the softness?

Where was Mrs. Ada?

Their chest tightened.

The grown-up helper came over. "Riley, come sit down."

But Riley couldn't move. Their feet were frozen. Their brain was spinning. Everything that made school feel safe was... gone.

"Where's Mrs. Ada?" Riley finally asked, voice shaking.

"She's home today, but she'll be back soon," the helper said.

Riley didn't feel better. "Why didn't anyone tell me?"

They rushed to the corner — but it wasn't the corner anymore.

Just tile. No rug. No stars. No magic.

"I want to go home," Riley whispered.

The helper nodded gently. "It's okay to feel upset. This was a big surprise."

Riley crouched down, arms wrapped around their head.

"I need something that feels mine," they said.

The helper quietly brought over Riley's fidget cube and a drawing from their cubby — the one with the tree, the sun, and the word "safe" written in orange crayon.

Riley took it slowly. Held it. Breathed.

Ms. Jenna came over and knelt down.

"I heard you love the old corner," she said. "Would it help if we found something soft to sit on? I can bring in pillows from the library."

Riley didn't answer — but they didn't turn away either.

By lunchtime, there were two star-shaped pillows in the corner. Not the same, but close.

Ms. Jenna gave Riley a soft smile. "I hope this helps a little."

Riley gave a small nod.

That afternoon, Riley sat in the almost-corner and read a book about birds that flew across the ocean — birds that sometimes got lost, but always found their way back.

Just like Riley was finding theirs.

Because change will happen — even the kind you didn't ask for.

But with time, patience, and people who listen...

new safe spaces can grow where the old
ones used to be.

Story 11: The Day Riley Broke the Routine

Flexibility, Panic, and Discovering Inner Strength

Every Wednesday, Riley's day looked the same.

Cereal for breakfast.

Green hoodie.

Music class second period.

Peanut butter sandwich at lunch.

Then home — to watch cloud videos before dinner.

It was safe. It was predictable. It was perfect.

But not today.

It started with the hoodie.

It was missing from the hook.

"I need my green one," Riley said.

"It's in the laundry," the grown-up replied. "You can wear the blue one today."

Riley blinked hard. "But it's Wednesday."

"I know," said the grown-up gently. "Let's just try this once."

Then music class was cancelled.

No drums. No shakers. No rhythm to follow.

Instead, the schedule board said "Guest Assembly."

The teacher called it "exciting."

Riley called it "wrong."

At lunch, the cafeteria ran out of peanut butter sandwiches.

They gave Riley a turkey wrap instead.

It smelled like pickles. Riley hated pickles.

Their hands were shaking. Their chest felt hot.

The walls looked like they were moving — tilting just slightly out of place.

Riley left their lunch on the tray and ran to the bathroom.

There, they sat on the floor, knees pulled up, hoodie (blue and too unfamiliar) bunched around their shoulders.

When the routine broke apart, Riley found shelter in stillness — and in someone who stayed without needing to fix.

"It's not Wednesday," Riley whispered. "Not anymore."

The grown-up came to find them.

They didn't speak at first — just sat outside the stall door, back against the wall.

Then they spoke in soft rhythms.

"Riley… you are here. You are safe. Your breath is still yours."

Riley listened. In, out. In, out.

"It's okay to be upset," the grown-up continued. "Everything felt too different. And you didn't get a choice."

Riley nodded slowly, eyes still closed.

When they finally stood up, the grown-up asked, "Do you want to come back to class? Or take your break space?"

Riley whispered, "Break space."

So they went there.

A soft room with low lights, calm music, and a blanket that smelled like lavender.

Riley wrapped themselves in the blanket, like a cocoon.

They didn't talk for the rest of the day. And that was okay.

When they got home, the clouds were still there — just like always.

They watched one drift by that looked like a green hoodie.

And Riley smiled.

Because even when the day falls apart — even when the plan is broken and everything feels upside down — Riley is still here.

Still whole.

Still worthy of kindness.

Story 12: Riley Learns It's Okay to Ask for Help

Support-Seeking, Emotional Safety, and Trust

Riley liked to figure things out alone.

They liked solving puzzles, finding hidden objects in books, and learning how things worked — especially on their own.

Independence felt strong. Safe. In control.

But today, something was different.

It started with math.

The numbers weren't staying still.

Riley's eyes felt blurry, like they were looking through fog.

The numbers just... didn't make sense today.

The teacher walked by and asked gently, "Need help with that one?"

Riley shook their head quickly. "I'm fine."

But they weren't.

Their stomach felt heavy. Their hands kept tapping the desk. The number 8 looked like a snowman that might fall over.

Later, in art, the paintbrush felt wrong in Riley's hand.

The bristles were too scratchy. The cup of water tipped a little and splashed on the table.

Riley didn't say a word. They just stared at their blank paper, waiting for it to disappear.

The grown-up came over. "Want me to help you rinse the brush?"

Riley whispered, "No." But their eyes were blinking too fast.

By the time they got home, everything felt tangled.

Riley dropped their backpack and sat on the floor — not in anger, just in silence.

The kind of silence that means "I don't have the words for this."

The grown-up sat beside them.

"You don't have to do everything by yourself," they said gently.

"I know," Riley said. "But sometimes I don't know how to ask."

The grown-up nodded. "Would it help if we practiced? Like… making a menu of ways to ask?"

Together, they made a list.

- "Can you sit with me?"

- "I feel stuck."

- "Can you help a little, but not do it for me?"

- "I don't know what I need, but I need something."

Riley smiled at that one. "That's my favorite."

The grown-up chuckled. "That one's pretty brave."

The next day, back at school, the same math problem showed up again.

It still didn't make sense.

Riley stared at it for a moment... then raised their hand halfway.

The teacher leaned in.

"I feel stuck," Riley whispered.

The teacher nodded once. "Let's work through it together."

And they did.

No fireworks. No big deal.

Just one tiny moment where Riley chose connection instead of pressure.

Because asking for help is not giving up.

It is reaching toward trust.

It is saying, "I matter enough to not carry this alone."

And Riley was learning that one small ask could bring big peace.

Story 13: Riley and the Mirror of Me

Self-Acceptance, Identity, and Celebrating Neurodiversity

Riley didn't always like mirrors.

Not because of how they looked — but because mirrors asked questions without saying anything.

"Why are you like this?"

"Why can't you be more like them?"

"Why is everything so hard sometimes?"

Riley didn't have answers.

But the questions still echoed.

One afternoon, Riley stood in the school bathroom, looking into the mirror.

They had just had a hard moment in class — the teacher changed the routine again, and Riley had frozen. Couldn't speak. Couldn't move. Couldn't explain.

Now, they were staring at their reflection, wondering if something was wrong with them.

The grown-up knocked gently.

"Want company?"

Riley hesitated, then opened the door.

They sat together on the bench outside the bathroom.

"I feel weird," Riley said quietly.

"What kind of weird?" the grown-up asked.

"Like… broken. Like a puzzle that's missing pieces."

The grown-up didn't rush to answer.

Instead, they pulled a small mirror from their bag. Not fancy. Just soft blue on the edges, smooth and calm.

"Look in here," they said.

Riley did.

"What do you see?"

Riley thought. "My face."

"What else?"

"My eyes. My hair. My tired."

The grown-up nodded. "I see your strength."

Riley looked again.

"I don't feel strong."

"Strong doesn't mean loud or perfect," the grown-up said. "Sometimes strong means showing up — even when everything feels heavy."

Different didn't mean broken — it meant Riley was growing strong in their own beautiful direction.

They sat quietly for a bit.

Then the grown-up said, "Do you know what I think?"

"What?"

"I think your brain is like a tree that grows sideways. It doesn't look like the ones around it — but it still reaches the sun. In its own way."

Riley smiled — just barely. "Sideways tree?"

"Yup. Beautiful. Unusual. Rooted."

That night at home, Riley drew a tree.

It curved left, then right. Its branches weren't even. Its leaves looked wild.

And at the bottom, they wrote:

"This tree is me."

Because being different is not the problem.

Feeling like you have to be the same — that's the heavy part.

But Riley was learning: they were not broken.

They were brilliantly built differently. And that was a story worth loving.

Story 14: Riley's Calm Down Superpower

Self-Regulation, Inner Strength, and Emotional Tools

Sometimes, Riley's emotions came in like waves during a storm.

Big. Loud. Fast.

One second, everything felt fine. The next? Too many sounds. Too many faces. Too many feelings crashing in at once.

Riley didn't always know why.

And honestly, they were tired of people asking.

But today was different.

It was art class — usually a safe space.

But someone spilled glue on Riley's favorite drawing.

The teacher said, "It's just paper. You can make another one."

Riley's throat tightened.

It was not just paper.

It was a dragon castle. With flying stairs. And it was perfect.

And now it was ruined.

Riley could feel the storm rising.

Fists clenched. Heart racing. Tears creeping close. A scream climbing its way up.

But then... Riley stopped.

Not because they weren't upset.

But because they remembered.

The Calm Down Superpower.

It wasn't magic.

It was the steps the grown-up had practiced with them — over and over.

1. Step Back.

Riley pushed their chair gently and stood up.

2. Breathe Out.

Three long, slow breaths — out of the mouth, like blowing wind across water.

3. Say the Words.

"I need a moment."

The teacher nodded, no questions. No fuss.

Riley walked to the corner with the soft blue mat and sat down. Hugged their knees. Closed their eyes.

Step 4:

Pick a picture in your mind.

Today, it was the sideways tree — Riley's tree.

The one with wild branches. The one that still reached the sun.

After a while, the grown-up sat beside them.

"Want to tell me what happened?"

Riley opened their eyes. "I was proud of that picture. It got ruined."

The grown-up nodded slowly. "That's really hard."

Riley didn't need fixing.

They just needed someone to get it.

Later that day, Riley made a new picture.

It was not a dragon castle.

It was a comic book page… titled:

"Calm-Down Powers: Used by Heroes Like Me."

And in the corner, drawn with pride, was a little kid with a hoodie, a breath bubble, and lightning in their eyes — not angry, just strong.

Because superpowers do not always roar.

Sometimes they whisper: I can pause. I can breathe. I can choose peace.

And that's exactly what Riley did.

Story 15: The Bravest Day of Riley's Life

Courage, Self-Belief, and Quiet Victory

The school was buzzing.

Today was "Show and Tell Day."

Kids were already lined up, holding their treasures — toy dinosaurs, family photos, musical instruments, a hamster in a tiny travel cage.

Riley sat in the back, fingers curled around their hoodie sleeve.

Their object — a rock from their special spot at the park — sat in their backpack.

Heavy. Safe. Untouched.

The teacher clapped her hands. "Who wants to go next?"

Hands flew up like rockets. Kids bounced in their seats.

Riley stayed still.

Their heart was thumping in their ears.

Their mouth felt dry.

Their brain whispered: Do not go. Just stay invisible.

The grown-up caught Riley's eye from the hallway.

They gave a tiny nod — not asking, not pushing. Just… reminding.

You can.

Not you have to.

Just — you can.

Riley slowly raised their hand. Not high. Just enough.

The teacher blinked, surprised — but smiled warmly.

"Riley? Would you like to share?"

Riley stood up slowly. Their feet felt like bricks.

They walked to the front. Opened their backpack. Took out the rock.

Everyone stared.

And Riley spoke.

"This is my rock. I found it after a hard day at the park. It's smooth, and it fits in my hand. When I hold it, my body feels a little quieter."

Bravery doesn't always look loud. Sometimes, it's a kid holding a rock and saying, 'This is me.

The room was still.

Riley kept going.

"I brought it because sometimes… brave doesn't mean loud. Sometimes brave is just showing up."

The teacher wiped her eyes.

The kids clapped softly — not too loud, not too wild. Just right.

And Riley smiled.

Not a pretend smile.

A real one.

After school, the grown-up gave Riley a hug that wasn't too tight.

"That was one of the bravest things I've ever seen," they said.

Riley didn't answer. They just held the rock in their hand — and knew.

Today wasn't perfect. It didn't need to be.

It was brave. It was honest. It was real.

And that made it the bravest day of Riley's life.

A Letter Just for You

Hey you.

Yeah — you.

If you're reading this, it means you've just walked through some pretty big stories.

Maybe you saw yourself in Riley.

Maybe your days sometimes feel like too much.

Too noisy. Too fast. Too confusing.

Maybe you've had moments when your body said "no," even if everyone else was saying "go."

I want you to know something right now...

That's okay.

Really, truly okay.

There is nothing wrong with needing quiet.

Or feeling overwhelmed.

Or walking away from something that doesn't feel safe.

That does not make you bad. That does not make you weak.

It makes you human.

It makes you you.

And you? You are not just okay —

You are brave.

Not the loud kind of brave.

Not the superhero-jumping-off-buildings kind.

But the kind of brave that whispers,

"I'm scared… but I'm still here."

"I don't want to do this… but I'll try in my own way."

"I need a break… and I'm allowed to take it."

That kind of brave?

It's the strongest kind there is.

So if your heart beats fast sometimes…

If your words feel stuck in your throat…

If you love big but need space too…

If your brain does things differently…

Guess what?

That's your magic.

And even when it feels hard, I want you to remember:

- You are not broken.

- You are not alone.

- And you are so, so loved — exactly as you are.

Riley found ways to breathe, speak up, and stay calm when things felt too big.

And you will too.

One small step at a time.

One soft breath.

One choice that feels safe for you.

This world needs kids like you.

So keep being you.

Because you are enough.

Always.

With all my heart,

Someone who truly sees you.

Parent & Caregiver Story Guide

A Companion to the Stories of Riley

Story 1: Riley and the Big Morning Storm

What it's about:

Routine disruption, sensory overload, and emotional shutdown.

Why it matters:

Mornings can feel like mini-battles for PDA children — especially when expectations suddenly shift. Riley's storm is not about defiance, but about the brain trying to regain control in a world that feels unpredictable.

Try this:

Offer "calm-down corners" before the meltdown. Talk about the signs your child feels a storm coming. Create a visual routine that includes room for flexibility.

Story 2: The Day Riley Did Not Want to Get Dressed

What it's about:

Sensory sensitivity and personal autonomy.

Why it matters:

PDA children often experience intense physical discomfort from clothes. Giving them choices, not commands, can make a world of difference.

Try this:

Build a "comfort drawer" with safe clothing options. Let your child decide what feels okay on their body. Avoid forcing clothing when resistance is high.

Story 3: Riley's Bubble of Calm

What it's about:

Creating internal tools for self-regulation.

Why it matters:

PDA kids thrive when they can imagine or visualize their own sense of calm. Giving them a "bubble" or "shield" can feel like giving them control back.

Try this:

Practice calm-down visualizations together when your child is already calm — so they'll be ready when things get big.

Story 4: Riley and the Lunchbox Mix-Up

What it's about:

Unexpected change and sensory-based food anxiety.

Why it matters:

Food routines are often sacred for PDA children. Sudden changes can feel violating and trigger panic.

Try this:

Validate your child's reaction. Offer a safe space to regroup. Avoid forcing "just try it" — this is not about pickiness, it's about safety.

Story 5: When Riley Wanted to Stay at the Park Forever

What it's about:

Transition struggles and the emotional weight of "leaving good things."

Why it matters:

Abrupt transitions can feel like loss for a PDA child. Having choice and ritual around endings helps them let go without panic.

Try this:

Create a "goodbye plan" together before outings. Use countdowns, final pushes/swings, or goodbye phrases to build closure gently.

Story 6: Riley's First Dentist Adventure

What it's about:

Fear of new environments, sensory overload, and the need for preparation.

Why it matters:

Appointments like dental visits can be deeply overwhelming — new faces, smells, sounds, and expectations. PDA children need control, predictability, and sensory safety.

Try this:

Use social stories, pictures, and even roleplay before the visit. Let your child bring comfort items. Keep the visit flexible and optional when possible.

Story 7: Riley Does Not Want to Say Hello

What it's about:

Social pressure, performance anxiety, and communication on their terms.

Why it matters:

Simple greetings can feel like demands. For PDA children, saying "hello" might trigger shutdown or fear of judgment. Respecting their communication style is essential.

Try this:

Teach alternative ways to greet (waves, drawings, nods). Help others understand that not saying "hi" is not rudeness — it's emotional safety.

Story 8: Riley and the Loud Birthday Party

What it's about:

Sensory overwhelm in social settings and using self-regulation tools.

Why it matters:

Busy, noisy, unstructured environments can be overstimulating and distressing. Riley's response shows that withdrawal is not avoidance — it's survival.

Try this:

Create an "exit plan" for parties. Pack sensory tools (headphones, fidgets, calm cards). Let your child choose how long to stay. Celebrate any participation as success.

Story 9: When Riley Does Not Want to Play

What it's about:

Social boundaries, emotional energy, and being misunderstood by peers.

Why it matters:

Kids with PDA are often social — on their own terms. When they need space, it's not rejection — it's regulation. Teaching this helps both the child and their friends.

Try this:

Help your child name their needs without shame. Offer scripts like, "I like you, I just need quiet right now." Support peer understanding through storytelling and modeling.

Story 10: Riley and the Big Change at School

What it's about:

Resistance to sudden change, grief over lost routine, and emotional safety.

Why it matters:

Change is hard for most kids — but for PDA children, it can feel dangerous. Their sense of control and trust depends on predictability.

Try this:

When possible, prep them in advance. If not possible, validate their emotions without rushing to "cheer them up." Rebuild safety one moment at a time.

Story 11: The Day Riley Broke the Routine

What it's about:

Overload caused by multiple routine disruptions and emotional dysregulation.

Why it matters:

When several things go "wrong" in a row, PDA children can hit emotional capacity quickly. Even small changes feel massive when trust in the day is broken.

Try this:

Avoid stacking demands when your child is already off balance. Instead, offer retreat spaces, familiar comforts, or co-regulation. Their meltdown is a message, not manipulation.

Story 12: Riley Learns It's Okay to Ask for Help

What it's about:

Support-seeking, internal pressure to cope alone, and trust-building.

Why it matters:

Many PDA children would rather struggle silently than ask for help — because help can feel like a demand or exposure. Asking is a huge step.

Try this:

Give your child multiple, low-pressure ways to ask — like hand signals, cards, or coded phrases. Celebrate the ask, not the performance.

Story 13: Riley and the Mirror of Me

What it's about:

Self-image, identity, and embracing difference.

Why it matters:

PDA children often feel "wrong" because they don't match the world's expectations. Seeing their difference as strength rather than flaw is life-changing.

Try this:

Create safe language around difference. Use metaphors (like the sideways tree) to help your child visualize their beauty and uniqueness. Affirm them often — not for what they do, but for who they are.

Story 14: Riley's Calm Down Superpower

What it's about:

Regulation skills in action, independence, and internal growth.

Why it matters:

This story shows progress — Riley doesn't need to be told what to do. They remember what helps. It's a reminder that consistency and safe practice lead to breakthroughs.

Try this:

Practice calming strategies during low-stress times. Give your child ownership over their own toolkit — and space to choose when to use it.

Story 15: The Bravest Day of Riley's Life

What it's about:

Speaking up, quiet courage, and self-expression.

Why it matters:

This moment isn't about perfection — it's about showing up when it's hard. PDA kids often struggle with public speaking or performance. This story celebrates a victory that belongs to them.

Try this:

Encourage expression without pressure. Let your child define what "brave" looks like to them — and recognize that for many, just trying is enough.

Loved This Book?

If Riley's story helped your child feel seen,

or gave you new ways to connect —

please leave a review on Amazon.

Your words help other families find this book

and remind the world that gentle stories matter.

Thank you for reading.

Thank you for caring.

Thank you for being here.

Made in United States
Troutdale, OR
04/29/2025

30994755R00069